"WHAT YOU OWE YOUR PARENTS"

*Thoughts on christian children's
response to their parents*

BENJAMIN TOMMY

To order additional copies of this book, contact:
Xlibris
1-888-795-4274
www.Xlibris.com
Orders@Xlibris.com

ACKNOWLEDGEMENT

This project is the handy-work of many dedicated faithful and committed brethren who have chosen to contribute in one way or the other. To begin:

I want to specially thank the Coordinator, Children Evangelism Ministry Int'l, Kaduna state and Zonal Director CEM Kaduna for his countless support in helping me to be where I am in this children ministry today and for also accepting to write the foreword of this book.

I also want to appreciate Mallam, Hassan Musa (PhD), a Lecturer with ECWA Theological Seminary, Kagoro for his zest, encouragement and irreplaceable tremendous insight played a critical role in the shape and content of this book.

I wish to also thank my colleague and friend Aunty Dorcas Luka for her all-round support to ensure that this work is well type-set for the Children and teenagers of this generation to read this book at ease.

I would like to thank my brother Kent S. Agang whose counsel has help in getting this book into the hands of our wonderful teens and children of our time.

I would also like to thank Mrs. Cynthia Ene Musa whom despite her tight schedule had accepted to edit this piece of work.

Similarly, I would like to say a big thank you to my wonderful relations, Promise, Daniel and Patricia who have been of great encouragement in writing the draft of this book.

I also wish to thank my Uncle Rev. Prof. Sunday B. Agang and Family for their unprecedented, spiritual, moral and financial support since my childhood who were and are always a parents and mentor to me in my difficult and happy moment.

To my loving and supportive Mother Mrs. Rhoda Kozah and Late Father, Mr. Tommy Duniyio Kozah, you deserve endless thanks for your patience and resilience in raising me up in the fear of the Lord to where I am today.

I must also thank my discipler Mr. Junias Avong for his willingness to help in contributing toward the contents of this book

Lastly, I want to say a big thank you to Dr. Mrs. Babatunde Oluwatope and Mrs. Rebecca Oyedele for their encouragement and acceptance to blurb over this piece of work.

A book like this depended greatly on the Leadership of the Holy Spirit. I am particularly grateful to God for the inspiration and strength to be able to write this book. Now *"To him who sit on the throne and to the Lamb be Praise and honour and glory and power, forever and ever!" Amen (Rev. 5:13).*

DEDICATION

I dedicate this book first to God Almighty for His strength and divine glorious unlimited resources in making this project a reality. And secondly, to God's chosen Children who are scattered all over the world.

FOREWORD

The Ten Commandments given to us by God through Moses is divided into three; man's duty to God, man's obligations to parents and man's duty to fellow man. The writer, who has been committed to the cause of Child Evangelism right from his school days, has specially packaged this book to enlighten our children/teenagers what their obligations should be to their parents.

Commandment number five made it clear that children must honour their fathers and mothers for their days to be long on earth (Eph. 6:1-2). This the author has enucleated to prescribe ways by which children must carry out their obligations to their parents.

Therefore, this book is recommended for children, teenagers and teachers of children, as a tool in combating the high level of coldness growing in the relationship between children, teenagers and their parents in our days (Proverbs 30:11-13).

Evang. Austin I. Edema

Coordinator, Children Evangelism

Ministry Int'l, Kaduna State and

Zonal Director CEM Kaduna zone.

ABOUT THE AUTHOR

Tommy D. Benjamin is a seasoned Children Minister and a writer of Children's articles. He graduated from Ahmadu Bello University, Zaria (ABU) where he obtained his Bachelor degree in Textile Science and Polymer Technology. He also obtained his Post Graduate Diploma in Education with Kaduna State College of Education Gidan Waya in affiliation to Ahmadu Bello University, Zaria. He was one time Children Evangelism Ministry (CEM) Campus Link leader, Ahmadu Bello University, Zaria. He had his Advanced Leadership Course with CEM in Management Personnel and Administrative Development (MAPAD). He is presently a staff with ECWA Theological Seminary Kagoro. Uncle Tom as is fondly called by many Children, currently lives in Manchok, southern part of Kaduna State.

ABOUT THE BOOK

This book seeks to help Christian teenagers and children to achieve their God-ordained obligations to their parents.

This book also intends to achieve the following objectives:

- ❖ To help both children and teenagers discovered their God given obligations to their parents.

- ❖ To enable children value their parents by giving them the maximum support they deserve

- ❖ To help children know that their obligation to their parents is not optional but a command from the Lord

- ❖ To expose both children and teenagers to know that their primary responsibility in the home is to obey God through their parents.

- ❖ Lastly the book also aims at bringing children back to their parents through a healthy and consistent personal relationship with God.

Hello Friends!

My name is Tommy Benjamin. Permit me to specially congratulate you for taking such a bold step in acquiring a copy of this book for yourself "**What You Owe Your Parents.**" I want to encourage you to keep the flame of God that is burning in you which is the Spirit of God. As we journey through the lines and pages of this book, I beseech you to open your heart to the great Teacher. That is the Holy Spirit, and you will have the best that this book intends to offer you with.

Finally, read this book calmly and prayerfully as you trust the Holy Spirit to enable you discover what you really owe your parents and how to help them in discharging your God given obligations to them and everyone around you.

Wish you a happy and successful reading in Jesus' name (Amen)!

INTRODUCTION

Do you know that you really owe your parents? Owing your parents simply means being indebted or obligated to them. There is nothing under this heaven and earth you will do for your parents that can be substituted or replaced with the love, care, protection, shelter, and the pains they passed through when they were carrying you. In fact, do you know there were times mummy and daddy couldn't sleep during the night nor eat and drink just to see you happy and doing better? Your mummy had every reason not to have carried you in her womb for nine months. Mummy and daddy did not think of aborting you, instead, they did their best to raise you to become the child that God wants you to be. You know why? It is because they did not only see you as a covenant child but have considered you as that perfect gift of God given to them as blessings.

Psalm 127:3 says that:

Sons are a heritage from the Lord, children a reward from him (NIV). It is actually a good thing to hear the Bible call us a heritage from the Lord (that is God's property) given to our parents as gifts and blessings from above. Well, you might ask, what do I really owe my parents? So, let's see what you owe them.

CHAPTER ONE

WHAT DO I OWE MY PARENTS?

To begin with, it is good you know that one of the most important things you owe your parent as a child or teenager is:

RESPECT

Respect means showing proper appreciation or regard for those who are in certain authority or position. Romans 13:7 says: ***"Give to everyone what you owe them…if respect, then respect, if honor then honor."*** It is God's original plan that we respect everyone irrespective of their class, age, religion; tribe, culture or even background. The word everyone simply means **ALL**. That is, to respect *"all people" or "everybody."* Does this include our parents? Yes! Now listen to what Leviticus 19:13 says: ***"Each of you must show respect for your Mother and Father…for I the LORD am your God."***

First of all, you need to know that you must respect your parents for the fact that they have cared and catered for your needs from infancy to the stage you are in now, whether you are a child or teenager. If you don't respect your parents, do you expect others to respect them? If you have not been showing them respect, then you have to change your attitude and start giving them the maximum respect they deserve. Otherwise you are absolutely not helping them or yourself. Come to think of this; is it a right thing to eat someone's food without thanking them? Or is it right to stay under someone's roof without paying or appreciating them? No! You need to show respect by appreciating all they have provided for you. Remember, as God's child, it is right to respect your parents who have brought you into the world and acknowledge their efforts by honoring them.

So, you can see that the Bible would have every child of God do what is right by respecting his parents. The question is, why would the Bible want us to respect our parents? There any consequences for not respecting them? The answer is absolutely YES. Now let us hear what **Ephesians 6:2b** has to say concerning this: **it reads:**

> *". . . Honor your father and mother.*
> *This is the first of the ten commandments*
> *that ends with a promise."*
> *Then you will live a long, full life in the land*
> *the LORD your God will give you." (NLT)*

What does this mean? It means honoring our parents has a reward. And what is the reward? "…***You will live a long, full life" (Exodus 20:12).*** This verse as well tells us that any child (boy or girl) who respects his or her parents will have blessed years on earth. That is, they will be fruitful (do well) and their lives will be free from regret.

As children of God, one of our goals is to make heaven. Do you think disrespectful children will go to heaven? You know that not all children live to their old age. Some children have died due to sicknesses, accidents, kidnap and other causes. In some cases, healthy looking children and youths have died silently on their beds without any symptom of illness.

Some of these children, like you, had great expectations. They thought of buying clothes, aero planes, cars and even building mansions for their parents when they grow up someday. Some died living sinful, and disrespectful lives to their parents and hence to God. What do you think would happen to those ones? **Go to HEAVEN**? No! I don't think so. Heaven is not for those who disrespect God. You may say I have never disrespected God and more over I read my Bible every day, go to church every Sunday and maybe go to Bible club. All these are good but that is not what I mean. The point is that any child who disobeys his parents is certainly disrespecting God. That sounds amazing, doesn't it? But that is true and God is not happy with that. You are not only to respect your parents because they gave birth to you, shelter you, pay your school fees, or even buy you goody-goodies, but you are to respect them because that is what God demands from you as His child. If you are a child or teenager reading this book, what God wants from you is to respect your parents and honor them. It is true that we earn the respect of others by respecting them, but as children of God, it is expected of us to respect our parents whether they have earned it or not. In other words if your father or mother doesn't seems to respect your decision or seem to be the kind of parents you wanted them to be, God still wants you to give them the respect they deserve. **1 Peter 2:17** says, *"Show proper respect to everyone."* Why should the Bible say that? It is because all human beings [small or big] are made in the image of God and therefore, are worthy of respect. In fact, verse 14 of Leviticus 19 put it clearly; **"Show your fear of God by not taking advantage of the blind."** Now it is very clear that God wants those who bear His name to respect everybody whether they are able or disabled people, Christians or Muslims, rich or poor, educated or illiterate or whatever they may be. Through this our light will shine and others will see Jesus in us and glorify God.

Also, Leviticus 19:32 says, ***"Show your fear of God by standing up in the presence of elderly people and showing respect for the aged."*** Do you know that Timothy in the Bible being a teenager, at the age of seventeen, had a Christian mother with an unbelieving father? He also had peers and friends but he did not allow himself to be influenced by them or to be looked down upon. In fact he did not allow that to make him disrespect his earthly father who was not a Christian. Timothy as a youth also grew in the midst of older men and women, young men and young ladies. Just imagine if Timothy did not respect his unbelieving father, do you think he would be able to show respect for others? Certainly Not! Respect does not come overnight. Charity begins at home they say and you cannot give what you do not have. So, as Children of God, God expects us to show respect to our parents at home for us to be able to respect others by relating well with them in church, school or public places. You might as well be reading this book and have not made Jesus your savior from sin; you are as well disrespecting God. No matter how hard you try to please Him and your parents you will not be able to, because your efforts cannot save you but Jesus can. And if you want to make Him your Savior I can help you do that. All you need do is to sincerely say this prayer;

Lord Jesus, I am a sinner; I have fallen short of your glory and have come to you for forgiveness. Please forgive me all my wrongs and write my name in the book of life and help me to honor you and my parents all the days of my life. In Jesus' name have I prayed (Amen).

Congratulations! You are now a child of God. You can do well by telling your parents, pastor or Sunday school Teacher about your new life in Christ. Please don't forget that, *"Jesus will never leave you nor forsake you"* (Hebrew 13:5b). Whenever you need His help which of cause you should, don't hesitate to call on Him. He will be very happy to come to your help.

HOW TO RESPECT YOUR PARENTS

Have you ever wondered why some youths and children are supported and favored both at home and outside? The reason is simple. It is because they respect their parents. **Malachi 3:17c** says, *"I will spare them as a father spares an obedient and dutiful child."* You might say your parents are different and somewhat hard on you. But I don't think so. The reason why some of our parents are behaving the way they do sometimes is because they don't like some of the things we are doing. And I can assure you that even God will support them for not putting up with such kind of nasty character. I hope you will be proud that your parents love you and they want the best for you. Now let us look at some of the basic things that we must do to our parents as signs of respect and obedience to them. The number one on the list is:

1. **Being grateful to your Parents**

   The Bible says that, **"He who is faithful over a little, much will be given to him"**. More so, the Bible tells us that; it is more blessed to give than to receive. Do you know that whatever you plant is what you will harvest? You can't plant maize and harvest yam. It is not possible! Now I want you to take a pause and think deep about this question: what are you actually giving to your parents? Are you giving them joy, peace, happiness and satisfaction or bitterness, anger, depression, pains and sorrows? Proverb 23:25 say: *"Give your parent's joy: and make them happy."* Remember whatever a man sows so shall he reap. Your little thank you to them can make them do more for you. Do you remember the story of Jesus healing the ten lepers' in the Bible? *Ten lepers were healed by Jesus but only one came back to say thank you to Jesus. And Jesus asked him were there not ten men healed? Where are the other nine?* You see even Jesus was not happy with their ungrateful character. He turned and said to the one that came back; go for your faith has made you well. You will agree with me that the leper who showed appreciation to Jesus will get more blessings than the other lepers. The more you show appreciation to God and to your parents, the more He would bless you.

HOW TO BE GRATEFUL TO YOUR PARENTS

You can also be grateful to your parents in the following ways:

   a. **By appreciating them for who they are and what they do**

   They may not be able to provide for all your needs but they would do their best for you. Remember that God allowed you to be born through them for a purpose. So learn to appreciate them.

Also, be grateful to them because they sacrificed their energy, resources and time to train you. Showing gratitude to your parents will make them do more for you.

b. Do not look down on them

Sometimes you feel your parents are old fashioned and don't know much but know this, what your parents want for you is right and the best for you. Listen to them and you will be blessed. Isaac blessed his two children-Jacob and Esau because they regarded him and they were blessed by God. If you must go far in life you need the blessings of your parents. The Bible says that with the blessings of the righteous a nation is blessed. You see every big tree today emanated from a small seed and every tall building had its foundation from the ground. So be humble, respect your parents and God will lift you up.

2. Value their wisdom

Your parents came to this world long before you were born and that means they know more than you do. You must note that they have passed through the stage you are in right now. Their experiences have helped them to be wise. If you desire to succeed in this world, you must listen to them and by so doing, you will grow in wisdom.

3. Be a wise child

Proverb 3:1 *says, a wise child is someone who accepts his parents' discipline.*

A wise child will always do the right thing at the right time as commanded by God and required by their parents. **Ecclesiastes 8:5b,** says that, *"Those who are wise will find a time and a way to do what is right."* Don't wait to be told on what to do. Check around you and see where you can help in the house. Most importantly, learn to ask the questions **What, When, Who, Why and How.** This I call **"4W+ H"**. These are compassed questions that will guide you to your destination.

For example when you wake up in the morning, you need to apply the **4W+H** by asking yourself these critical questions.

First W=What am I supposed to do? ...... (Dress my bed, tidy the house and do other chores required of me)

Second W=When am I supposed to do it? .... (Every morning and at the time stipulated by my parents)

Third W=Who will do it.................... (I will do the chores)

Fourth W= Why must I do it?........(I want to make my parents happy and to keep the house clean)

H=How will I get it done? Knowing that my parents will be happy means I have a blessing from God. I can do everything through Christ who gives me strength.

These questions are applicable to all kinds of activities. Be it academics, profession, business and even boils down to personal life's problems and challenges. If you identify the cause of the problem and commit them in prayers to the Lord then it is solved. Jesus said, whatsoever you ask in my name it shall be done unto you. The word whatsoever means anything you ask that is according to God's will shall be done unto you.

4. **Be an honest child**

Honesty is the attitude and practice of telling the truth. "Jesus said, "I am the way, the truth and the life" (John 14:6). That means any person that say the truth has Jesus in him and Jesus is with him. And in Matthew 5:39 Jesus also said, ***let your 'Yes' be 'Yes' and your 'No' be 'No.'*** Jesus demands we tell the truth at all times. You know why? John 8:31-32 says, *"You shall know the truth and the truth shall set you free."* So anyone that does not tell the truth is not free from the bondage of the Devil that is why he tells lies. And Jesus said, "You are like your father the Devil who is a liar. Choose to be a child of God by being an honest child otherwise you will bear the consequences of telling lies. Dishonesty leads to:

a. **Lack of trust:** Someone who tells lies cannot be trusted

b. **Eternal hell:** Revelation 21:8 says, ***".....the idolater and all liars their place will be in the fiery lake of burning sulfur."*** That is Hell fire.

Always say the truth even when it may mean punishing you. But it is the right thing to do. If you do that, God will certainly honor your courage and reward your faithfulness. Remember Joseph in the Bible, he chose to please God by not submitting to Potiphar's wife demands and God honor him while he was in prison.

5. **Never follow the crowd**

Never follow the crowd just because you want to please someone. You cannot please everybody but you can make God happy. Please choose to do the right thing and avoid bad friends. Associate with people that believe what you believe in and became what you want to become. Remember, a friend of thief is also a thief. Proverbs 23:22 says, ***"listen to your father who gave you life, and don't despise your mother's experience when she is old."***

6. **Follow the good teaching of your parents**

Proverbs 3:1-4 says:

"¹ My child, don't forget what I teach you. Always remember what I tell you to do. ² My teaching will give you a long and prosperous life. ³ Never let go of loyalty and faithfulness. Tie them around your neck; write them on your heart. ⁴ If you do this both God and people will be pleased with you."

If you follow your parent's rules (teachings and instruction) you will certainly save yourself from a lot of punishment and regrets in the future. Rules are not bad. They are guides that protect you from unforeseen dangers that may arise. God gave Adam and Eve rules to obey in the Garden of Eden; they were warned not to eat the forbidden fruit but they disobeyed and got punished. God also gave us rules one of which is to respect our parents but if we disrespect them, we will have to bear the consequences all the days of our lives.

7. **Learn to say sorry**

Quickly tell your parents sorry whenever you learnt that you have wrong them or did not follow their instruction. Be honest and sincere when apologizing to them. And the Bible also added that, in everything we should do it without grumbling and arguing. This is what God wants from His Children

8. **Be humble and take Correction**

True humility and fear of the LORD lead to riches, honor and long life, says the Bible in (Proverb 22:4).

The main essence of correction is to help us see well, think right and act correctly. It is also a mirror that shows you what your two eyes and instinct couldn't see. And don't be angry when you get corrected by your parents or someone. Proverb 23:19 reads: ***"My Child, listen and be wise. Keep your heart on the right course*** and Proverb 3:11 says:

> [11]***"My child, don't ignore it when the LORD disciplines you,***
>
> ***and don't be discourage when he corrects you***
>
> [12]***for the LORD corrects those he loves, just as a father***
>
> ***corrects a child in whom he delights. So be happy whenever***
>
> ***you got corrected."***

How do you feel whenever you made a mistake most especially, when writing on your book? You feel great? I don't think so! Am sure you feel very sad and disappointed especially if it was a work that you have expended a lot of energy. Sometime you feel as if you shouldn't continue with the work but when you take your time to erase it well using corrective fluid or eraser, it looked pretty good and made you feel better. The entire work might look excellent and beautiful when it is done on a separate sheet though it may cost you an extra paper, the work would certainly be awesome. This is exactly what correction does to any child who accepts it. It makes you a better person than what you were. I am sure if you see it as your mirror; you will never have a cause to regret in life.

9. **Pray for your parents**

Prayer is a means of talking to God, and God talking back to us. To be able to fulfill your God's given duty to your parents, you have to learn to pray. Otherwise you will find yourself always struggling whenever you try to do it. Luke 18:1 says, ***"Men ought always to pray and not to faint.*** It means without prayer we will become so weak in obeying God's word.

Our parents are not always right but that does not mean we should disrespect them. Don't always complain about them for not understanding with you. Thank God that you know where they need help. Getting upset with them can't change anything. But you can do something thing for them that changes everything which is, prayer. Matthew 7:7 says,

> ***"Keep on asking, and you will be given what you ask for,***
>
> ***keep on looking, and you will find. Keep on knocking***

and the door will be opened. For everyone who asks receives.
Everyone who seeks, finds. And the door is opened for everyone
who knocks. Don't lose hope. Keep on praying and the LORD
will answer you." (NLT)

10. <u>**Help your parents**</u>

The Bible say as arrows are in the hand of a mighty man so are the children of the youth (Psalms 127:4). But why should the Bible compare us to an arrow? The reasons are very clear. They are:

a. **Small but very powerful**

Do not belittle yourself. Though you may look small physically but know that you are strong. The Bible also mentioned that, "As you think so are you." That is whatever you call yourself is what you will become. If you say you are small you will be small and if you say you are strong you will certainly be strong. It doesn't matter what people calls you, but what matters the most is what God says you are. Gideon saw himself as a weakling but God told him that he was a man of courage. In other words, God was telling Gideon that he was a strong man. He believes God and succeeds.

More so, the Bible says that, "Let the weak say I am strong and the poor say I am rich. Frankly speaking, David in the Bible was a little boy when he confronted Goliath- in fact he was like a little ant compared to what Goliath looked in terms of height, body posture, weight and strength. But David did not look down on himself nor was he discouraged when his own brothers ridiculed him at the battle ground. Instead he was strong and went in the Might of God. Alas! The mighty Goliath was killed by the so called "little boy". God also wants you to stand for Him in your family by fighting for the truth as David did so that God's righteousness will fill up everywhere on earth. You can do this by also helping your parents at home.

b. **An arrow travels far**

Who can decide your destiny? No one! Not even your teachers, friends, relations and even your enemies. But only God can do that. That is why you and I must respect Him by protecting our parent's weaknesses if we must go far in life. Remember Jabez in the Bible? His story was told in the book of 1 Chronicle 4:9-10, that:

"There was a man named Jabez who was more distinguished than any of his
brothers. His mother named him Jabez because his birth had been so painful.
He was the one who prayed to the God of Israel, "Oh, that you would bless me
and extend my hands! Please be with me in all that I do, and keep me from
all trouble and pain!" and God granted him his request."

Do you think God can also grant your request by changing your destiny? Of course He will. He is a loving and caring God.

IMPORTANCE OF SHOWING RESPECT

Do I stand to benefit anything by respecting my parents? If that is your question I want to tell you that you stand the chance to benefit a lot from obeying your parents. Some of these things are:

1. **Recognition:** Showing respect to our parents is a way of recognizing their achievement and what they have done for us. Guess what? That will bring you a lot of recognition wherever you go.

2. **Care:** Showing care to others shows we care about them. Whenever we do that, others will care about us too.

3. **Getting respect ourselves:** How can we expect others to respect us unless we respect them.

4. **Mankind:** We should respect each other because we are all created in the image and likeness of God.

SECTION ONE: QUIZ QUESTIONS

1. A grateful child does not appreciate his parents for who they are and what they do TRUE/FALSE

2. A child that is grateful to God for His parents will never look down on his parents TRUE/FALSE

3. He who is faithful over a little, much will be given to him TRUE/FALSE

4. A respectful child always give his parents joy and make them happy TRUE/FALSE

5. A respectful child always listen to his parents advice and instruction TRUE/FALSE

6. Dishonesty leads to lack of trust and eternal condemnation TRUE/FALSE

7. God's child does not say sorry TRUE/FALSE

8. 4W+H are compassed questions that guide us to our destination. What do they stand for?

9. If we love our parents we will pray for them TRUE/FALSE

10. If we respect our parents we will help them TRUE/FALSE

11. When we care about others, others will care about us TRUE/FALSE

12. Respect brings shame TRUE/FALSE

13. When we respect our parents others will respect us TRUE/FALSE

CHAPTER TWO

OBEDIENCE

This leads us to the second thing we owe our parents. Do you know that obedience is more than following a list of **"Do's** and **Don'ts"?** *Obedience is simply doing what you are asked to do it at the time and manner in which you were asked to do it. In other words, it simply means doing one's duty.*

More so, your obedience to your parents should not and must not only be based on what you have to gain by doing all the **Do's** or by observing all the **Don'ts** in order to save yourself from the punishment of breaking it but instead, it should be that you are doing it to please God. Jesus said, *"I have come to do your will, O God"* (Hebrews 10:7). And it is also God's will for us to obey our parents. This is the example we are to follow be it in thoughts, actions and in every aspect of our lives. Therefore, we are to obey our parents in the Lord.

There are three important reasons why God wants us to obey our parents. The first amongst these is that:

a. **Obedience is right**

Obedience is the right thing and best thing to do. It is an order set by God for all His children to follow. There is a saying that says "Obedience is the first law in Heaven." No wonder, Lucifer (who we now call Satan), was not permitted to stay in Heaven when he disobeyed God by breaking one God's commandments. Let us see the sin he committed against God in **Isaiah 14:12-16.**

¹²How art thou fallen from Heaven,

O' Lucifer, son of the morning!

How art thou cut down to the ground,

which didst weaken the nations!

¹³For thou has said in thine heart,

I will ascend into heaven,

I will exalt my throne above the

Stars of God: I will sit also upon the

Mount of the congregation, in the

sides of the North:

¹⁴I will ascend above the heights

Of the clouds; I will be like the Most
High.
¹⁵ Yet thou shalt be brought down
To hell, to the sides of the pit
¹⁶ They that see thee shall narrowly
Look upon thee, and consider thee,
Saying, is this the man that made
The earth to tremble, that did shake
Kingdoms;

From where we have read, Satan or Lucifer did not only want to be like God, he wanted to be God. He never wanted to obey God and the result was disgrace and ejection from heaven. So, you must see that the consequence of disobedience is very great. Jesus, though being God did not think of himself highly above God, the Father, but obeyed His earthly parents and God's will even unto death.

Jesus had to do what he did because; obedience is the right thing to do. Do you know that even non living things who have no life and brain know how to obey? The sun was to govern by day and the moon to rule at night as commanded by God were and are still doing their jobs to this day and they have never changed even for once. Young animals are also taught to obey. For example the chicken's chicks are always under the protection of their mother. She provides them with food and water, the disobedient chicks are picked up and devoured by the hawk if they veer off from her protection but the obedient ones are kept safe and unharmed. You see, it's good we learn from these animals and obey our parents.

b. **Obedience is a Command**

Another reason why we should obey our parents is that obedience is a command from God to all Children. **Command is an instruction that must be carried out**. Mind you, it is not an instruction that **MAY BE DONE** but an instruction that **MUST BE DONE**. Remember, anything that must be done that is not done will always attract a penalty (punishment). **Ecclesiastes 8:5a** says that *"Those who obey... will not be punished."* When God was giving the ten-commandments to the Israelites through Moses, He also included all children (that is, children from all ages) provided you are under your parents you must obey them. He instructed them in Exodus 20:12 by saying, ***"Children honor your father and mother: that your days may be long upon the land which the LORD your God will give you.***

To honor them means much more than to obey them; it also means showing them great respect. The verse one and two of the chapter six of Ephesians in the Good News Bible made it clear when it says *"Children, it is your Christian duty to obey your parents, for this is the right thing to do. Respect your father and mother."* ***Obedience is more than doing what you are asked to do: it is simply fulfilling your God's divine purpose in the lives of your parents as God will have you do.*** Your obedience is not complete if it is conditional. It must be out of willingness; don't say if my parents will be this or that, or do this and that then I will respect and obey them. God would not be happy with you if you do such things. But learn to obey them not only because they are your parents but because God has commanded it to be so. One of our popular songs said it all when it says:

O-B-E-Y

Obey Jesus Command

O-B-E-Y

Make Him very glad

Listen to the word He says

Obey Jesus every day,

O-B-E-Y

Obey Jesus Command.

If you do this, your parents will be proud of you and most importantly, God will be pleased with you.

Finally, you can bring honor to your parents by the way you live. Listen to what **Proverbs 1:7-8 says:**

The fear of the Lord is the beginning of knowledge,

but fools despise wisdom and discipline.

Listen, my son, to your father's instruction and do not

forsake your mother's teaching.

(NIV)

Be a wise child. Fear the Lord and heed to your parent's instruction for it shall be an ornament of grace unto your head, and chains about your neck. What this scripture is saying is that the Lord will act on your behalf, honor you, and His covenant of love will be upon you (that is, God's promises and blessings will be all yours) because you heed to your parent's advice. And if you honor them, you will love them and care for them. If you truly respect them you will not walk out on them when they are talking to you. In fact you will not use any profane word or body language that is not God glorifying when talking to and with them. Instead, with humility and calmness you tell them sorry. If you are a hot tempered person, you can ask God to take it away from you. I remember back then in primary school, how I found it so difficult to control my temperament most especially, when people jibed (insulted) at me. One day someone tried my patience, before I knew it, I already bounced at his nose with a blow. Guess what? The worst happened! I remember how I felt bad deep inside me and how I told God sorry and that I want Him to take it away from me. Guess what? God did it for me. It was not magic. God can also do it for you if you allow Him to help you.

Lastly, Jesus said, **"When you obey me, you remain in my love, just as I obey my father and remain his love. I have told you this so that you will be filled with my joy. Yes your joy will overflow!** (1 John 15:10-11). So it is clear that, only those who are obedient can have the joy of the Lord. When David disobeyed God and killed his commander, Uriah and married his wife. God was not pleased with what David did. From that day God took his joy from David. After this, David prayed to God to restore to him the joy of His salvation (Psalm 51: 12). God did same to Saul when he failed to kill the king of the Amalekites and also kept some animals to be sacrificed to the Lord even though the Lord asked him to destroy everything. It is clear that half obedience is **Not** obedience at all. Whenever we choose to live a disobedient life, we will never experience God's joy in our hearts. The Bible says, *"The joy of the Lord is your strength"* (Neh 8:10).

"It is possible to work in obedience. If we put our hope in God and continue to trust in Him, He will give us His strength that comes from His joy to overcome all kinds of sins that so easily entangle us." Do you love Jesus? If you love Him you will keep His commandment by obeying your parents.

1 John 5:2-4 say it all:

> *"We know we love God's children if we love God and obey His commandments. Loving God means keeping His commandments, and really, that isn't difficult. For every child of God defeats this evil world by trusting Christ to give the victory."*

c. <u>**Obedience Bring Blessings**</u>

Do you know that life on earth would have been unjust, unfair and practically of no use if it has no reward (blessing)? Do you also know that God would have been considered a partial God if he had not punished Satan for his disobedience? God wouldn't have been a God of justice if the righteous and the wicked are given the same reward. Read what God said on this in the book of Malachi 3:16-18.

> *[16] Then those who feared the Lord talked with each other,*
>
> *and the Lord listened and heard. A scroll of remembrance*
>
> *was written in his presence concerning those who feared the*
>
> *Lord and honored his name.*
>
> *[17] "They will be mine," says the Lord Almighty.*
>
> *"on the day when I act, they will be my own special treasure,*
>
> *I will spare them as a father spares an obedient and dutiful child.*
>
> *[18] And you will again see the distinction between the righteous and the wicked,*
>
> *between those who serve God and those who do not."*

For more emphasis verse 18 says *"And you will again see the distinction between the righteous and the wicked, between those who serve God and those who do not.*

Wow! What really is the distinction between the righteous and the wicked? **Malachi 4:1b-3** reads:

> *All the arrogant and every evildoer will be stubble [that is burned up], and that day that is coming will set them on fire," says the Lord Almighty."Not a root or a branch will be left to them.[2] But for you who revere [that is respect] my name, the sun of righteousness will rise with healing in its wings. And you will go out and leap like calves released from the stall.*

³ Then you will trample down the wicked; they will be ashes under the soles of your feet on the day when I do these things, "says the Lord Almighty.

The difference is that, the righteous will not be destroyed on the day of God's judgment, and so it is with every child that obeys his parents. **Ephesian 6:3** says, *"It will be well with you and that you may live long on earth"*

From this portion of the scripture, we have two wonderful promises that God has for His children who obey their parents. They are:

a. **Good life**

If you read that same **Ephesians 6:3** in the opposite way it says, *If you don't obey your parents it will never go well with you*

b. **Long life**

This does not exactly mean that, those who obey their parents may not die young nor did those who died young actually disobey their parents. It only means that if you obey your parents you will have a complete life here on earth and you will also live eternally (that is for thousands upon thousands of years) with God in heaven, when He returns because **Ecclesiastes 8:13** says that *"The wicked will never live long, good lives, for they do not fear God."* However **Ecclesiastes 8:12** reads that…*"Even though a person sins a hundred times and still lives a long time, I know that those who fear God will be better off."*

In summary, life is not measured by the quantity of time (number of years in which you lived) but by the quality of life you lived. Jesus lived for about thirty three years on earth before He ascended into heaven. But what he did during those years were remarkably magnificent such that if the whole books of the earth were to be gathered, they **CANNOT** and **WILL NOT** be able to carry all the good things that Jesus did while He was on earth. The disciples of Jesus also did many great things while they were alive, same with Elijah, Samson, John the Baptist and many others which space will not permit us to discuss about them.

SECTION TWO: QUESTIONS

1. Obedience is not a command TRUE/FALSE

2. Command is an instruction that must be carried out TRUE/FALSE

3. Obedience is doing one's duty/work TRUE/FALSE

4. Those who obey will not be punished TRUE/FALSE

5. The sun, moon and the stars also obey God TRUE/FALSE

6. The two wonderful blessings of obedience are 'Good life and Long life' TRUE/FALSE

CHAPTER THREE

REPRESENTATION

The third thing you owe your parents as a child of God is "representation." Representation is the act of standing in for somebody. It also means to act or speak...for somebody and defend [protect] their interests. And this is exactly what God needs you do for Him and your parents.

Do you know that any person that goes to the market, hospital or school does that for a purpose? In fact, any child that is born to his parents is also born for a purpose! And what is the purpose? That he, represent his parents by living a life of good character. But how can we do this? This question now leads us to:

HOW TO REPRESENT YOUR PARENTS

Do you really desire to represent your parents very well? If 'Yes', then all you need now is to have the right attitude. Philippians 2:5 says that, ***"The attitude you should have is the one that Christ Jesus had."*** This is the attitude I am talking about. Listen to Philippians 2:2-4. It reads:

*² **I urged you, then to make me completely happy by having the same thoughts [that is attitudes], sharing the same love, and being one in soul and mind. ³ Don't do anything from selfish ambition or from a cheap desire to boast, but be humble toward one another, always considering others better than yourselves. ⁴ And look out for one another's interests, and not just for your own.*** Now I would like you to kindly pause here for a while as you take your pen to write down some of these attitudes that these verses want us to have in the space below:

1……………………………………………………..

2……………………………………………………

3……………………………………………………

4……………………………………………………

Please make sure you fill this space and make it your prayer before turning to the next page. Now let's continue with our discussion. Why do you think the Bible encourages us to have these attitude? Because it is...**"The nature of God"** (Philippians 2:6b). Understand that it is God's will that we carry His nature which is His attitude. Having these attitudes simply means you are speaking for God or defending His interests and that means you are as well representing your parents.

Now let's see how we can represent our parents in other areas of life. One of these is the:

School

School is a good place to be. Sometimes it could be fun and sometimes it could be bored. We all had these experiences at a certain time in our lives. The amazing thing is that we are all there to represent God and our parents. Jesus said that, *"You are the light of the world"* (Matthew 5:14a). He did not say that the world is the light but "YOU" are the light to the "world." This is good news isn't it? Jesus wants you to show forth his light in your school. It is one of those reasons God did not allowed us to school in anyhow school but the very one you are schooling. God knew that you can make others to be like him when we pray for them; when we show them more love and care; when we support them with what we have or by the way we live with others. It is when we practice these that God can be glorified in us.

Do you also know that one group of the people in the society that deserve respect from us, our parents, and the communities are our teachers? They did a good work in making our society a better place. Through them we gain knowledge and develop skills that make us useful people in the society. Do you know that we can represent our parents well in school when we respect and obey our teachers because of the efforts they made in teaching us? Have you ever taken time to imagine the time and energy your teacher used to prepare games for you, to instruct you in your lessons, to watch and direct your progress and to also make sure you become a student of good character? It is true that you pay school fees; but your teacher's love and blessing can never be measured in terms of money.

When we respect and obey our teachers, they become motivated to do their duties and help us learn well. A humble child will therefore, represent his teacher and parents.

If we obey our teachers in school we will do well in life. It is in our interest that we obey and respect our teachers if we must succeed. Whatever the subject you are offering in school, if you have no respect for your teacher you may probably make no progress unless you carefully follow their instructions.

A good student doesn't disobey their teachers: Remember at one time that your teachers had been students themselves. Your difficulties and trials had been theirs. They know what is good for you better than you know yourselves. Their love for you, their desire for your progress, their joy in your destination, and the pain you cause them when you err, is as great as, if not greater than, that of your parents. If you are sure of this as you ought to be, will you disobey your teachers? Now ponder on what happened to this man in a far away land:

Long ago, it came to the notice of the school that some students often urinate on the wall of the school instead of going to the school toilet. One day the school disciplinary committee decided to post a bill on the school wall that reads: **DO NOT URINATE HERE!** After many days, Schur, one of the senior students was caught by his class monitor urinating on the school wall. Schur pleaded and promised never to repeat it. Two days later after the acts, Schur went back to the same place where everybody was cautioned not to pee and urinated. What do you think will happen to Schur? Would he be pardoned or reported? This time around Schur was not pardoned but reported to the school management. Guess what? Schur had to pay for his disobedience. As such he was punished by the school authority.

After many years of graduation, Schur contested to be president of his dear country. What do you think will happen? Lose the election? Not at all! He won the election as many people voted for him. Four days to the swearing-in of the elected president, the Electoral Tribunal gave out a three-day ultimatum for any person who has a genuine reason, with a proof of evidence why the president elect should not be sworn as this had been the custom of the country's election. Shocking, on the day of the swearing-in, the attorney General of the country called out again for the last time for any misconduct or criminal acts found that will render the election void. As Schur was standing beside the Chief Lawyer of the federation to be installed as the elected president, there was an instant silence in the president's court, where the ceremony was taking place as everyone turned to see whether anyone had any charge against the president to-be. Within the twinkle of an eye, a man appeared from the back and said, with all honor your majesty, "I have a petition against the elected president. Table it for the Tribunal is listening" said the Chief Lawyer. "Thank you my lord. The man standing before you was my classmate in our middle school days and I was their class monitor. I stand here to tell the general assembly that this man is not worthy to be the president of our beloved country for a reason like this: This man you see here before you was convicted for a breach of conduct and disrespect to the school authority. And here is the evidence, my Lord!" When the magistrate looked upon the petition and found out that Mr. Schur was guilty, he was disqualified immediately by the tribunal. Thus, he lost the seat of the presidency. This is what disobedience can cause us. Hence, our action today may affect our future tomorrow just like Mr. Schur. Though he changed, he had to face the consequences of his past action.

However, here are some few tips that can help us represent our parents well in school:

1. **Go to school early:** If you go to school early you will not only save yourself from punishment, but you will also save yourself from a lots of embarrassment and distractions in the class. Guess what? You will have enough time to organize yourself in the class and to also ask relevant questions that will help improve your understanding on every subject you are taking.

2. **Do your home work:** If you do your home work by yourself you will not need to be afraid of anything that may arise in the class. In fact you can be sure that you have done more than half of your work as a pupil or student.

3. **Read your books:** Kurt Schmoke, became a youngest former state attorney for the city of Baltimore [that is the chief lawyer] of the United State of America. He once said to the students of his former school: *"Read. Read books. That is how to get someplace in life"* If you read your books today you will not only be somebody tomorrow; you will also be a better person than you were. This is what Ben Carson has to say on this: "Learning is not always easy, not always fun or appealing, but is necessary." Who was Ben Carson? One of the brilliant students in his class? No! He was one of the dullest pupils in his school days. He was mocked and jeered by his class mates in school. But today is one of the most successful medical doctors in the world to have operated on the human brains. When he started reading his books he knew that "he has a brain." But the first time he started reading he said that reading was never easy, it was never fun-but it was necessary for him to read. May be someone once told you that you just can't know anything and that had probably become a problem to you. Do not worry about that anymore. I have got some good news for you. Jesus said, *"To him who believes nothing will be impossible for him to do."* Do you believe you can be somebody tomorrow? Yes, you can! Philippians 4:13 reads *"**I can do everything through Him who gives me strength.**"* Does that have to do with your studies in school? Yes, be it Mathematics, English, Basic

science, Biology, Geography, Chemistry or Physics. Whatever the subject may be, the Bible says you can do everything. The word **'everything'** means no exception provided it is God's will. Guess what? It is also God's will that you do well in school. Look at what God said: *"My people perish for lack of knowledge"* (Hosea 4:6). Who are the people? They are those who believe in Christ. The word "knowledge" simply means *"to know."* You see it is God's will that you do not only know Him but that you also know what you are doing both at home and in school. The problem is, why do people [children, teenagers and adults] perish for lack of knowledge? Jesus said you do not receive because you do not ask. Ask that your joy may be complete. It is now very clear that Jesus wants you to have a complete joy in whatever you are doing. And James 1:5 says, *"If you need wisdom- if you want to know what God wants you to do-ask him, and he will gladly tell you. He will not resent your asking. But when you ask him be sure that you really expect him to answer, for a doubtful mind is as a wave of the sea that is driven and tossed by the wind."* Do you lack the wisdom in knowing what you are being taught in school or elsewhere? Feel free to ask God who is your father to give you wisdom. God wants you to ask but you must not doubt when asking. Otherwise you will not receive any anything.

4. **Pay attention to your teachers:** It only when we listen we can learn well. James 1:19 asserts, be slow to speak but be quick to listen.

5. **Ask questions when you need clarity:** Those who ask questions never get lost. Jesus said, "Ask and it shall be given to you." If you want a solution to your problem then you have to start asking questions now.

6. **Avoid unnecessary play in the class:** An idle man is the Devil's workshop. Get something doing otherwise you will be a nuisance in the class.

7. **Dress neat:** When God was to talk to the children of Israelites He commanded them to wash their clothes and appear neat before Him. You see even God is a Holy God as such, He dislikes dirtiness. Remember, cleanliness is next to Godliness.

8. **Avoid cheating or exams malpractice:** The number eight of God's commandments says, "Thou shall not steal." As a child of God you are not supposed to steal someone's pen, crayon, book or cheat during exams. Why? Because stealing is a sin and God hates sin. So learn to hate sin too by not compromising your faith in God. Proverbs 21:5 says *"Good planning and hard work lead to prosperity but a hasty short cut leads to poverty."* Don't look for easy way. Bend down and read and you too will also be successful. You got the brain!

Don't envy others when you see them practicing all forms of malpractice in school and are passing well. Deuteronomy 6:7 says, *"The Lord your God is a faithful God, keeping His covenant of love."* Just be strong, the Lord will keep His covenant and reward your decision.

9. **Avoid fight:** God's children don't fight. You are not to fight in school for whatsoever reason. If anyone offended you, instead of taking a fight you can do well by reporting him or her to your class teacher or the appropriate authority. If you do that it means that you are strong and God will be happy with you. Sometimes people may forcefully take what is yours to see what you can do; sometimes they may even accuse you of what you did not do, or ask for a fight from you to see if you are strong enough. When they do all these to you and feel tempted to fight them back,

just look up to God for help and he will give the strength to overcome these temptations. Do you think God will not hear you? He will! The Bible said the ears of the Lord are open to the cry of His children. And He will rescue those who are in trouble. God want to rescue you. He will be happy if you allow him to help you. Guess what! If you do all these, your teachers, parents and God will be pleased with you.

10. **Participate in class or group discussion:** Do your best to contribute to the group you are paired to work with. It could be in the home, church, school or any gathering. No matter the how small or big that group is, there is something you can do. Do not belittle yourself. Maybe you are thinking you are the smallest person in the group, or maybe you are thinking you know nothing. Sometimes it could even be that you think you know better than your other group members. No matter what you may be feeling or thinking about God will not be happy if we refuse to share our fears or knowledge with others. Imagine you are the only person in the world with no one to talk to, no one to share your pains or joy with, and no one to curdle you or laugh with. How will you feel? You will definitely feel unhappy. Life on earth will not be fun. Whenever we participate in a class or group discussion we do not only feel happy but also learn.

11. **Respect other people's opinion:** It is not all the time we are right. Sometimes we get things right and sometimes we get things wrong. Whichever way it is good we learn to appreciate other people's thought. God always want us to learn from others because they have something that we do not have. Nobody is all-knowing except God.

Church

The Church is also another place where people gather together to worship God. The Sunday service should not be taken for granted. It must be respected. Don't skip church service to do something else that will not be God-glorifying. Except for some genuine reasons otherwise avoid been idle. They say an idle man is the devil's workshop.

The Bible says that, "whoever comes to God must believe that He is the rewarder of those that diligently seek Him." Whenever we appear before God we are to do away with anything that may be a distraction to us. Your friends, cell phone, chocolate, chewing gum, dressing or even your problems could also be a distraction to you. God will not come and take them away from us. We are the ones to do that. If you are sincere and faithful in seeking the Lord, He will certainly bless you. Remember God blessed Solomon with wisdom when he sought Him sincerely from his heart. If you take God seriously He will certainly bless you. The Bible says, "Blessed are they that come in the name of the Lord." What this verse is saying is that, those who come to God sincerely will not only be blessed with happiness but it shall also go well with them physically, socially, mentally and spiritually.

We can represent God in the Church when:

1. We give thanks to God in every situation

2. We pay attention to His Word in the church

3. We dress well

4. We avoid eating or chewing of goodies in the Church

5. We avoid roaming around

6. We come with our Bible and writing material.

Public Place

There are different types of people in the world. Some are good others are bad. **Luke 6:45 says, *"A good person produces good deeds from a good heart, and an evil person produces evil deeds from an evil heart. Whatever is in your heart determines what you say."*** The people we live with, the friends we keep, the places we go the things we eat and the things we look have much effect on our lives. They will either make us **good people or bad people.** The Bible says, "Bad Company corrupts good manners." And that is why the Bible tells us that we should come out from among them and be separated. God doesn't want His children to mix with the world, even though they are in the world but are not of the world.

More so, Romans 12:2 says, ***"Don't copy the behavior and customs of this world, but let God transform you into a new person by changing the way you think. Then you will know what God wants you to do, and you will know how good and pleasing and perfect his will really is."*** People around you may tempt you to copy their bad way of talking, dressing and even the way they think but instead, let your attitude towards dressing, thinking and living be like that of Christ. You can only do this by reading, praying and living God's Word.

Lastly, you need to walk with God's children if you really desire to represent God here on earth and to also make your parents happy. You don't have to worry because you are not alone on this journey. Jesus said: *"I am with you always, even to the end of the age."* (Matthew 28:20b) and Jesus also said in Revelation 3:5 that, ***"All who are victorious will be clothed in white. I will never erase their names from the book of life, but I will announce before my Father and his angels that they are mine."***

If this book has really helped your life, I will like to hear from you. You can reach me on: tommyben91@ gmail.com

SECTION THREE: QUIZ QUESTIONS

1. A good student does not disobey his teachers TRUE/FALSE

2. A good student go to school early TRUE/FALSE

3. A good student does his home work TRUE/FALSE

4. A good student study his books TRUE/FALSE

5. A good student pay attention to his teachers TRUE/FALSE

6. A good students ask questions if he doesn't understand TRUE/FALSE

7. A good student does not dress neat TRUE/FALSE

8. A good student does not participate in exams malpractice TRUE/FALSE

9. A good student does fight in school TRUE/FALSE

10. A good person does good things from his heart TRUE/FALSE

11. An evil or bad person does bad things from his heart TRUE/FALSE

12. We represent God when we give thanks to Him in every situation TRUE/FALSE

13. We represent God when we pay much attention to His Word TRUE/FALSE

14. We represent God when our dressing glorify Him TRUE/FALSE

15. We represent God when our thoughts and actions pleases God TRUE/False

16. We represent God when we don't roam carelessly TRUE/FALSE

QUIZ ANSWERS

Section one

1. F 6. T 11. T

2. T 7. F 12. F

3. T 8. What, why, when, where, how

4. T 9.T 13. T

5. T 10. T

Section two

1. F

2. T

3. T

4. T

5. T

6. T

Section three

1. T 6. T 11. T 16. T

2. T 7. T 12. T

3. T 8. T 13. T

4. T 9. F 14. T

5. T 10. T 15. T

BRAIN TEASER/MEDITATION

1. **(i) What do you owe your parents?**

_____

_____

_____

(ii) Why do you owe your parents?

_____

_____

_____

2. **(i) If respect is showing proper appreciation for those who are in authority or position, then how should we respect our parents?**

_____

_____

_____

(ii) What can you do to respect your parents?

_____

_____

_____

(iii) Why should you respect your parents?

_____

_____

_____

(iv) How can you respect your parents?

_____

_____

_____

3. **What habit must you stop today to if you must represent God and your parents?**

_____

_____

_____

4. **What must you do to become a good student?**

_____

_____

_____

5. **Who is a good student?**

_____

_____

_____

6. **What is obedience?**

_____

_____

_____

7. **Why must you obey your parents?**

_____

_____

_____

8. **How can you obey your parents?**

_____

_____

_____

9. **When can you obey your parents?**

_____

_____

_____

10. Where can you obey your parents?

_____

_____

_____

11. What are the consequences of disobeying your parents?

_____

_____

_____

12. What are the rewards of obedience?

_____

_____

_____

BIBLIOGRAPHY

1. *Growth THOTS Teacher's Manual,* A Guide for Children Teachers in Churches, Schools and Clubs, Volume 13

2. *The Biblical Illustrator,* Ages Software, Inc. and Biblesoft, Inc.) Commentaries on: Ephesians 6:1-4; Ephesians 6:1-4 Copyright © 2002, 2003, 2006

3. Bridges, J. *The pursuit of holiness,* USA, Oasis International Limited, 2008

4. *Advanced Learner Dictionary,* Eight Edition, Oxford

5. Liardon, R. *The School of the Spirit,* Kaduna, Evangel publishers, 1994

SCRIPTURE INDEX

CHAPTER ONE

Romans 13:7
Leviticus 19:13
Ephesians 6:2b
Exodus 20:12
1 peter 2:17
Leviticus 14:19
Leviticus 19:32
Hebrew 13:5b
Malachi 3:17c
Proverbs 23:25
Proverbs 3:1
Ecclesiastes 18:5b
John 14:6
Matthew 5:39
John 8:31-32
Revelation 21:8
Proverbs 23:22
Proverbs 3:1-4
Proverbs 22:4
Proverbs 3:11
Matthew 7:7
Psalm 127:4
1 Chronicle 4:9-10

CHAPTER TWO

Hebrew 10:7
Isaiah 14:12-16
Ecclesiastes 8:5a
Exodus 201:12
Proverbs 1:7-8
1 John 15:10-11
Psalm 51:12
Nehemiah 8:10
1 John 5:2-4
Malachi 3:16-18
Malachi 4:1b-3
Ephesians 6:3
Ecclesiastes 8:13
Ecclesiastes 8:12

CHAPTER THREE

Philippians 2:6b
Matthew 5:14a
Ephesians 4:13
Hosea 4:6
James 1:5
James 1:19
Proverbs 21:5
Deuteronomy 6:7
Luke 6:45
Romans 12:2
Matthew 28:20b
Revelation 3:5